The world remains confused, and lacks understanding regarding the culture of the Middle East. *Escaping Islam* is a provocative and timely story that is rich with historical events, giving the reader verbal exposure to the dangers brought about by Iran's support of radical Muslim ideology.

Mano Bakh was a high ranking officer in Iran's Imperial Navy when, in 1979, during the Islamic revolution, he miraculously escaped with his life. The harrowing experiences he was subjected to, currently exemplifies the free world's necessity to deal with the ongoing aggressive Islamic movement, and the oil money that supports it. This living story begins with an introduction to Iran's history and Persian customs. It continues by encompassing the development of OPEC, the amazing Khark Island oil project in the Persian Gulf, and relating the happy life of a young boy growing up in his grandmother's house in Tehran. Tunnels connected the homes of the thirty two family members who enjoyed the daily ceremony of dining together around an antique Persian carpet, adorned with a white Sofreh, "table cloth," while grandmother smoked her water pipe.

* * * * * * *

Mr. Bakh was born a Muslim, but became disenchanted with the religion whose mission was to kill or convert all who did not believe in the teachings of the Koran. His candid understanding of what happened to a country that was once America's best friend and then turned into an *Axis of Evil,* will educate the reader as to why that Evil might not be realized until it is too late.

Joy, laughter, prosperity, hope and respect in Iran's society, quickly changed to hate, revenge, misery and mourning!

Escaping Islam

The Evil Might Not Be
Realized Until It Is Too Late

To Michael
With Regards.

Mano Bakh

A living story by

Mano Bakh
Kelli McIntyre
Jacqueline Le Beau

authorHOUSE®

AuthorHouse™
1663 Liberty Drive, Suite 200
Bloomington, IN 47403
www.authorhouse.com
Phone: 1-800-839-8640

First published by AuthorHouse 2/9/2009

ISBN: 978-1-4389-4156-1 (sc)
ISBN: 978-1-4389-4157-8 (hc)

Printed in the United States of America
Bloomington, Indiana

This book is printed on acid-free paper.

Kelli McIntyre's Biography

Kelli McIntyre attended Tulane University, where she double-majored in History with an emphasis on the Holocaust and World War II, as well as, African and African Diaspora Studies with a focus on the Civil Rights movement. Her passion for history and the rights of victims led Ms. McIntyre to seek a career in the law. Since graduating from Tulane School of Law, Kelli McIntyre has dedicated her career to the prosecution of criminals and protection of victims' rights. Ms. McIntyre is a member of the bar in both California and Louisiana and has worked as a district attorney in both states. Ms. McIntyre's legal career's predominant focus is on preventing the exploitation of children for sexual offenses, and violent crimes in the United States.

Ms. McIntyre became involved in the biography of Mano Bakh after learning of his remarkable life, and his goal to end the recruitment of all people, especially the children who are seduced into becoming suicide bombers. Using cultural insights acquired through Mr. Bakh's own life experiences, he has created an elaborate plan to end the egregious practice of self-sacrificing children, and young adults, in the name of Allah. This message is in keeping with Ms. McIntyre's life's work and drew her support to this powerful project.

Acknowledgments

It has been my pure luck and destiny to meet and get acquainted with a man who influenced me a great deal and encouraged me to write this book. He was William Le Beau, whom I carry a great respect for. I regret he did not live to see his sway. His wife, my dear friend Jacqueline Le Beau, has shown me her patience and elegance in everything she has done to help bring this book to fruition along with the talents of her granddaughter Kelli McIntyre.

Mano Bakh

Contents

Dedication

I am a man of seventy years, an American, one of many who was taken in by a great country in my time of need. I was born a Persian and lived in an era within my own country, Iran, that continues to be questioned. I hope I will be remembered as a person of principle, who has tried to live by what is right with respect for those whose lives I have encountered. None of us know how our actions will be interpreted. This is all that I ask for as I dedicate these memoirs to my children.

I know that my motivation to survive through all of my struggles was because of my love for my beautiful children. It is important to me that they, and all those who come after them, know who they are and where they came from, along with the part I played in the destiny of their birth country. This story is about my life and their heritage and hopefully will become their frame of reference.

Mano Bakh